Thematic Poems, Songs and Fingerplays

45 Irresistible Rhymes and Activities To Build Literacy

by Meish Goldish

CONTENTS

Cover design by Vincent Ceci
Cover illustration by Sue Woollatt
Interior design by Jacqueline Swensen
Interior illustration by Jan Pyk

Adapted from THEMATIC POEMS, SONGS AND FINGERPLAYS by Meish Goldish.
Copyright © 1994 by Scholastic Inc. Reprinted by permission of Scholastic Inc.
This edition © Scholastic Ltd 1997.
ISBN 0-590-53779-2

INTRODUCTION

Welcome to *Thematic Poems, Songs, and Fingerplays!* Integrating these irresistible verses into your curriculum will delight children and give them opportunities to discover the richness of language. They are also an ideal instructional tool for introducing or reinforcing thematic learning.

The reading and chanting of poems and fingerplays or the joy of a sing-a-long provide shared-reading experiences in which all children can be successful. These rich opportunities also develop the sense of being part of a community of readers and help to build important early literacy skills such as:

- ◆ understanding the concept of word;
- ◆ recognising words by sight;
- ◆ noticing language patterns and rhymes;
- ◆ connecting sound to print; and
- ◆ learning about directionality, spacing, and other components of print.

Thematic Poems, Songs, and Fingerplays offers many ways to empower children and foster a love of learning. Opportunities to participate in small groups or perform individually will develop a spirit of cooperation and build self-esteem. Invitations to embellish a selection by creating a prop or playing a simple musical instrument will spark creativity. And more good news: These poems and songs offer a natural extension for creating new verses or encouraging other kinds of writing.

Each of the poems and songs in this book includes a special page filled with ideas for reading the selection and extension activities.

The verses themselves can be presented in a number of ways. For example, you might copy them onto a large sheet of paper, prepare transparencies for the overhead projector, or provide children with individual photocopies – it's up to you and the needs and interests of your children. There are many ways to use *Poems, Songs, and Fingerplays*, but only one rule: Have fun!

GREEN PLANTS

(sung to "Three Blind Mice")

Three main things, three main things,
Green plants need, green plants need.
For plants to grow, for plants to thrive,
In order to keep green plants alive,
What does it take so they'll survive?
Three main things!

Plants need sun, plants need sun,
That's number one, plants need sun.
For plants to grow, for plants to thrive,
In order to keep green plants alive,
What does it take so they'll survive?
Plants need sun!

Plants need air, plants need air,
Be aware, plants need air.
For plants to grow, for plants to thrive,
In order to keep green plants alive,
What does it take so they'll survive?
Plants need air!

Plants need water, plants need water,
'Specially when it's hotter, plants need water.
For plants to grow, for plants to thrive,
In order to keep green plants alive,
What does it take so they'll survive?
Plants need water!

Suggestions for Sharing

◆ Let the children hold up one, two, and three fingers as they sing about the first, second, and third needs of green plants. They may also form their arms in a large circle to represent the sun, wave their hands about to represent air, and wiggle their fingers in a downward motion to represent water.

◆ Organise children into three groups. After everyone sings the first verse together, let each group sing a subsequent verse. While singing, children may first crouch down and then slowly rise, to suggest a growing plant.

Thematic Activities

◆ To demonstrate the three needs of green plants, take two green plants. Leave one where it will get no water, no sunlight, and little air. Give the other plant all three elements. Let children observe the plants daily and describe how they begin to differ in appearance over time.

◆ To demonstrate how green plants take in water through their roots and into their leaves, add red food colouring to a glass of water. Place a fresh stalk of celery with leaves attached in the coloured water. After a few hours, point out how the colouring has made its way to the celery leaves.

LIFE OF A BUTTERFLY

(sung to "The Incy Wincy Spider")

A butterfly begins
By laying all her eggs.
Out pops a caterpillar
Crawling on its legs.
The caterpillar first is
Very, very thin,
But it eats and eats and eats
Till it bursts out through its skin!

Soon the caterpillar's
Grown nice and big.
So it climbs on top
Of a tiny leaf or twig.
It makes a hard shell
And there it hangs inside.
The shell soon cracks
And then the parts divide.

Now here's a fact
That's really, really strange:
Inside the shell
There's been a major change!
When the shell opens,
What comes out?
A beautiful butterfly
Fluttering about!

Suggestions for Sharing

◆ Let the children use their fingers to imitate the movements of the caterpillar in the song. For example, they may wiggle one finger to show the caterpillar crawling, and open their hand wide to show the caterpillar "bursting" through its skin.

◆ They could use cupped hands to represent the caterpillar's hard shell then open their hands to show how the shell divides, and flap their hands to show the butterfly flying away.

◆ Tell the children that the hard shell is called a cocoon.

Thematic Activities

◆ Use a science book to show pictures of a butterfly at different stages of its development. Organise children into four groups. Then offer each group a large sheet of paper on which you've printed one stanza or portion of a stanza of "Life of a Butterfly." (Hint: Divide the first stanza of the poem into two parts, with one part representing the butterfly laying eggs and the other part representing the caterpillar popping out of the egg.) Invite groups to paint or draw their assigned stage of development. When all illustrations are complete, place the pages together between two additional pieces of paper. Punch three holes down the left-hand side of the sheets and use ribbon or looseleaf rings to bind the pages together into a big book. On the cover of the book, create overlapping butterfly shapes by tracing around pairs of children's feet with different coloured crayons. Print children's names on their butterfly wings.

◆ Ask children to describe different kinds of butterflies they have seen. Let each child draw a large picture of a beautiful butterfly and then cut it out. Fold the wings to make the butterfly look like it is flying.

TIME FOR HIBERNATION

(sung to "Frere Jacques")

Are you sleeping, are you sleeping,
Big brown bear, big brown bear?
Time for hibernation. What is your location?
In a log, in a lair.

Are you sleeping, are you sleeping,
Little frog, little frog?
Time for hibernation. What is your location?
In a pond, near a log.

Are you sleeping, are you sleeping,
Hanging bat, hanging bat?
Time for hibernation. What is your location?
In a cave is where I'm at.

Are you sleeping, are you sleeping,
Slinky snake, slinky snake?
Time for hibernation. What is your location?
In the mud, in a lake.

Are you sleeping, are you sleeping,
Turtle friend, turtle friend?
Time for hibernation. What is your location?
In the stream, till winter's end!

Suggestions for Sharing

◆ Assign some children to be the animals in the song and other children to be the chorus. The chorus sings the first three lines of each verse, leaning their heads on their hands to indicate sleeping. Then let the animals respond by singing the last line of each verse.

◆ The children can use socks to create instant puppets corresponding to the animals featured in the song. They could use a brown sock to represent the bear, a grey sock to represent the snake, green socks to represent the frog and the turtle, and a black sock to represent the bat. Cut extra body parts (eyes, legs, wings, shell, and so on) from construction paper and tape them to the bases of the socks. The children can then take turns using the puppets to sing the song.

Thematic Activities

◆ Let the children create a mural that shows the homes in which various kinds of animals hibernate. On long sheets of lining paper, they could draw pictures of caves, logs, ponds, streams, and other places where animals rest for the winter. Then ask them to find pictures from magazines of the animals and paste them into their proper homes.

◆ Help the children to learn more facts about animals and their hibernation habits. Then ask them to record and illustrate their findings in a hibernation book. First, suggest they draw hibernating animals on paper and then show them how to conceal the animals with sticky notes decorated to resemble hibernation hiding spots.

ANIMALS IN DANGER!

CHORUS:
Danger! Danger!
Animals in danger!
Animals in danger
May not survive.
Help them! Help them!
We want to help them!
We want to help them
Stay alive!

The Bengal tiger,
The mountain gorilla,
The African elephant,
The whooping crane.
The California condor,
The Asian rhinoceros,
We want to help them
All remain!

CHORUS

What can we do
For animals in danger?
What can we do
So they'll survive?
Never, ever hunt them,
Never take their homes away.
That is the way
They'll stay alive!

Suggestions for Sharing

◆ Help the children to find pictures of each animal mentioned in the poem. (Encyclopedias, children's nature magazines, and non-fiction books on endangered species are all good sources for animal pictures.) Ask the children to draw pictures of the animals on cards, which they can hold up as they recite the poem.

◆ Let the children cover their faces with their hands as if in distress, during the first four lines of the chorus. Then let them hold their hands out, as if offering help, during the last four lines.

Thematic Activities

◆ Talk about the reasons why animals become extinct (hunting, loss of habitats, difficulty mating in foreign environments, pollution, and so on). Let the children brainstorm ways they can help to protect animals. Record all their ideas. Also, write a class letter to a wildlife conservation group requesting additional ideas that the children might implement, and add these to your list. Decide together on one idea to pursue as a group (reducing waste, conserving water, collecting money to donate to a charity, and so on). Decide on a way to keep track of your efforts.

◆ Ask the children to imagine what two or more endangered animals might say to one another if they could talk. Let them work in pairs to create a conversation and perform it for the class.

CITY LIFE, COUNTRY LIFE

(sung to "Yankee Doodle")

Farmer Johnson has a home
Way out in the country.
There are fields and hills and lakes,
And apples grow on one tree.

Farmer Johnson likes her home
In the country quiet.
Through the fields she'll often roam,
And says that you should try it!

Mister Nitty has a home
In the busy city.
Streets and people all about,
And buildings tall and pretty.

Mister Nitty likes his home
Near the city's action.
Going all about the town,
It gives him satisfaction!

We can learn from Farmer Johnson
And from Mister Nitty.
Some folks like the country life,
While others like the city!

Suggestions for Sharing

◆ Suggest that the children listen carefully to a line-by-line recitation of the poem so they can decide on motions to help turn the poem into a fingerplay. For example, children may decide to wiggle their fingers upside down to indicate "roaming" through the country and the city.

◆ Organize the children into two groups: the country people and the city people. Offer members of each group index cards which may be punched through with a hole puncher, strung with wool, decorated with pictures of the country or the city, and worn as medallions. Let the country people sing the first two verses, the city people sing the second two verses, and both groups sing the final verse together.

Thematic Activities

◆ Let the children discuss how life is different in the country to that in the city. Ask them to give reasons why they would rather live in the country or the city. Create a large chart to record their responses.

◆ Let the children cut out magazine pictures to create collages of country scenes and city scenes. Title the collages "What We See in the Country" and "What We See in the City."

HOMES ALL AROUND

(sung to "Home on the Range")

Oh give me a home
With a snow-covered dome,
In an igloo that's cosy in sleet.
Or just let me stay
In a house made of clay,
An adobe is cool in the heat.

Homes, homes all around,
In the world, many homes can be found.
A palace or tent,
An apartment to rent,
In the world, there are all kinds of homes!

Now some people float
In a house on a boat,
And in tepees they live with no floor.
And some homes are built
Very high on a stilt
So the river won't rise to the door.

Homes, homes all around,
In the world, many homes can be found.
A cabin of logs,
Or a doghouse for dogs,
In the world, there are all kinds of homes!

Suggestion for Sharing

◆ Let the children use their hands and arms to suggest the details in each verse of the song. For example, they may put their fingertips together to form an igloo's dome. When the children sing the chorus, let them make a circular, sweeping motion with their arms to suggest "homes all round".

◆ Help the children find pictures of the homes mentioned in the song. Let them hold a picture each to show at the appropriate time during recital.

Thematic Activities

◆ Let the children use blocks, cardboard, clay or other materials to build a model home. The model may be just one room or an entire dwelling. Later, let individuals display their work and describe the kinds of homes they've made. As an alternative activity, the children may simply draw pictures of their homes.

◆ Help children locate the places on a world map where igloos, adobes, tepees, houseboats, grass huts, yurts, and other types of homes can be found. Pin a small picture of each kind of home to its proper place on the map.

WE ARE ONE WORLD

Pierre lives in Canada,
Maria lives in Spain.
But both like to ride their bikes
Along a shady lane.

Liv lives in Norway,
Ramon is in Peru.
But both laugh with the giraffe
When visiting the zoo.

Anwar is Egyptian,
Kim is Japanese.
But both run beneath the sun
And fly kites in the breeze.

Jack is from the U.S.A.
Karintha is from Chad.
But both write a poem at night
Upon a writing pad.

Children live all over,
The world's a giant ball.
But far or near, it's very clear
We're one world after all.

Suggestions for Sharing

◆ Display a large world map on the classroom wall. Let the children stand next to the map as they recite the poem and point to the places that are mentioned in each line.

◆ Help the children make flags of each country mentioned in the poem. Then, during the recital, the children can wave their flags as the appropriate countries are named.

Thematic Activities

◆ As a class, research the countries mentioned in the poem as well as other countries of interest. Then work together to create a We Are One World big book. If you like, each child can write and illustrate a page.

◆ The children can learn from older family members where their relatives may have lived before coming to this country. Pin an index card with the name of each child on the appropriate country on a large world map. Encourage volunteers to share interesting stories they have heard about relatives immigrating or adjusting to their new homes.

THE RAINFOREST

(sung to "Pussycat, Pussycat")

Rainforest, rainforest,
Covered with trees,
Home to the monkeys
And parrots and bees.
Rainforest, rainforest,
Who else is there?
Butterflies, toucans,
And bats in the air.

Rainforest, rainforest,
Covered with green,
Flowers and ferns
Like the world's never seen.
Rainforest, rainforest,
What's on the ground?
Lizards and pythons
Are creeping around.

Rainforest, rainforest,
Covered with rain,
Growing the plants
That we hope will remain.
Rainforest, rainforest,
Why do we care?
To make sure the rainforest
Always is there.

Suggestions for Sharing

◆ Let the children use their hands and fingers to imitate the movements of the rainforest creatures moving about. For example, fluttering hands can represent butterflies and bats, while creeping fingers can represent pythons and lizards.

◆ Help the children to decide on different rhythm instruments that can be used to represent the various rainforest animals and rain in the song. For example, a triangle might represent a butterfly, and sandblocks could represent pythons and lizards. After the children decide on their roles, they should begin playing their instruments when their animals or the rain is mentioned in the song and keep playing until the song's end.

Thematic Activities

◆ Let the children make their own model rainforest in the classroom. Using a large cardboard box or plastic tank as the base, put in grass, leaves, twigs, insects, and other examples of plants and animal life. Let the groups of children create special habitats for the animals who might live in their rainforest.

◆ Talk about the current debate over whether or not rainforest trees should be cut down. Explain both sides of the issue (developers' needs versus the preservation of rare plants and animals), and let the children express their opinions. They could write to a local or national environmental organisation for more information on the topic.

THE SOLAR SYSTEM

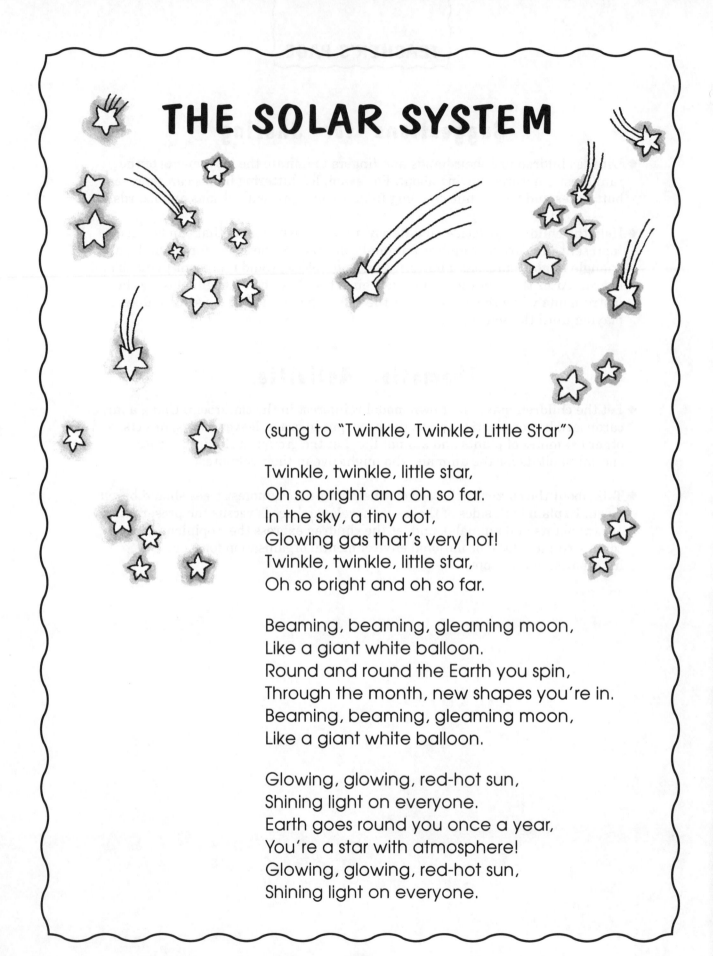

(sung to "Twinkle, Twinkle, Little Star")

Twinkle, twinkle, little star,
Oh so bright and oh so far.
In the sky, a tiny dot,
Glowing gas that's very hot!
Twinkle, twinkle, little star,
Oh so bright and oh so far.

Beaming, beaming, gleaming moon,
Like a giant white balloon.
Round and round the Earth you spin,
Through the month, new shapes you're in.
Beaming, beaming, gleaming moon,
Like a giant white balloon.

Glowing, glowing, red-hot sun,
Shining light on everyone.
Earth goes round you once a year,
You're a star with atmosphere!
Glowing, glowing, red-hot sun,
Shining light on everyone.

Suggestions for Sharing

◆ Divide the class into three groups: stars, moons, and suns. Let the children make cardboard representations of their heavenly bodies to wear as they perform the song.

◆ All the stars form a large circle, with the moons and suns standing inside. During the first verse, the stars wave their arms to represent twinkling. During the second verse, the moons walk·around the inside of the circle to represent orbiting. During the third verse, the suns spin slowly to represent rotation.

Thematic Activities

◆ Make a class mobile of the solar system. Children may use items such as tinfoil balls, yellow tennis balls, and ping pong balls to represent the stars, sun, moon, and the planets. Hang each item from string tied to the ceiling to create a giant solar system.

◆ Encourage the children to look for the moon every night for a month in order to draw its changing configerations. (Hint: Try offering copies of reproducible blank calendar pages so they can easily record their moon observations.)

MACHINES

(sung to "The Wheels on the Bus")

The wheels on machines go round and round,
Round and round, round and round.
The wheels on machines go round and round,
Whirring their sound.

The pins on machines go ping, ping, ping,
Ping, ping, ping, ping, ping, ping.
The pins on machines go ping, ping, ping,
Pulling the spring.

The rods on machines go side to side,
Side to side, side to side.
The rods on machines go side to side,
See how they slide.

The pulleys on machines go up and down,
Up and down, up and down.
The pulleys on machines go up and down,
High off the ground.

The screws on machines go twist, twist, twist,
Twist, twist, twist, twist, twist, twist.
The screws on machines go twist, twist, twist,
Twist like your wrist!

Suggestions for Sharing

◆ Let the children use their arms, hands, and fingers to simulate the different movements of the machine parts. For example, their hands can circle "round and round," their fingers can point "ping, ping, ping," and their arms can slide "side to side."

◆ Assign a different machine part to each child or group of children. Let them all stand side by side. After each child or group has sung its individual verse, let the entire class sing all the verses simultaneously, to give the impression of all the machine parts working together.

Thematic Activities

◆ Let the children talk about the different machines they use each day, such as alarm clocks, radios, refrigerators, and cars. Let each child draw a picture of a particular kind of machine they rely on. Use the pictures to create a collage entitled "Machines We Depend On."

◆ Encourage each child to invent a new kind of machine, such as a bed maker or a homework solver. Children may draw pictures of their inventions or make actual models. Let them display their inventions and describe what they do and how they work.

SAFETY FIRST!

(sung to "Skip to My Lou")

CHORUS:
Rules, rules, stick to the rules,
Rules, rules, stick to the rules,
Rules, rules, stick to the rules,
Stick to the rules for safety!

Look both ways when crossing the street,
Cars must make a stop complete,
Use your eyes before your feet,
Stick to the rules for safety!

CHORUS

Don't light matches, it's no game,
Things can quickly catch aflame,
Fire spreads, and that's a shame,
Stick to the rules for safety!

CHORUS

Never run by a swimming pool,
You could slip and be a fool,
Walk instead and play it cool,
Stick to the rules for safety!

CHORUS

Don't throw stones that you have found,
You might hit someone around,
Leave them safely on the ground,
Stick to the rules for safety!

CHORUS

Suggestions for Sharing

◆ Let the children imitate the action in each verse of the song, emphasising the right ways to behave. For example, they may pretend to be looking both ways before crossing, putting down a box of matches, walking by a pool, and leaving stones on the ground.

◆ Each time the chorus is sung, the children wag their index fingers as if giving a warning about not following the rules.

Thematic Activities

◆ Talk about important safety rules to observe. Then let the children, work individually or with partners to create large posters advertising critical rules of safety, such as "Look Both Ways Before Crossing". Encourage the children to illustrate their posters. Display all work prominently in the classroom.

◆ Invite guest speakers to your class, such as a fireman/lady, a lifeguard, and a lollipop man/lady to discuss the importance of safety rules. Encourage children to prepare questions to ask each guest during the visit.

BUILDING A SNOWMAN

Roll a snowball on the ground,
Roll it till it's big and round,
Pack the snow—pound, pound, pound!
That's the bottom of your snowman!

Roll a second ball of snow,
Roll and roll and watch it grow,
Plop it on the ball below,
That's the middle of your snowman!

Start to roll just one more ball,
Make it round but slightly small,
Place on top—don't let it fall!
That's the top of your snowman!

Use a button for each eye,
A carrot nose you then apply,
Place a hat on way up high,
You've got yourself a snowman!

Suggestions for Sharing

◆ Let the children imitate the actions in the poem by "rolling" their hands as if making a snowball. Also let them "pound" the snow and then lift it with their arms.

◆ You may wish to organise the children into four groups. As they recite, let one group make the first snowball, another make the second, another make the third, and the last group add the items to the head.

Thematic Activities

◆ Offer the children white or beige clay dough and invite them to roll the clay into balls and skewer the balls onto toothpicks to create clay snowpeople. Snowpeople may be decorated with scraps of fabric or paper, bits of plastic (toothpaste-tube caps make ideal snowpeople hats) or foil, or twigs. Snowpeople may then be placed together on a large mirror resting flat on a table or desktop. Twigs pressed into additional balls of clay can serve as wintertime trees, and a sprinkling of soapflakes or wisps of cotton may be added to complete the wintery display.

◆ Talk about how snow feels when it is used to make a snowman. Let the children compare snow to other building materials such as mud, clay, sand, and brick. How are they alike? How are they different? Create a comparison chart that lists the similarities and differences between snow and other materials.

WHAT TO WEAR?

What to wear? What to wear?
It all depends on the weather.
Look outside, then decide.
Here, let's do it together.

Pitter-patter! Pitter-patter!
See the rainy sky.
Wear your raincoat and your boots
To keep you nice and dry!

Hooray, hooray! A sunny day!
Let's play by the pool.
Wear a lightweight shirt and shorts
So you'll be nice and cool.

Yo ho! Yo ho! A blanket of snow!
Last night there was a storm.
Wear a coat, a scarf, and gloves
And boots to keep you warm!

Whoosh! Whoosh! Poor little bush!
The wind is making it sway.
Wear a sweater when you go out
So you don't catch cold today!

Suggestions for Sharing

◆ Organise the children into four groups and let each group dress to match one of the verses of the poem (excluding the first verse). One group may dress in raincoats and boots, another group in light-weight shirts and shorts, and so on.

◆ Let the children recite the first verse together. Then let each group step forward when reciting its own verse. Children may peform actions such as holding umbrellas, fanning themselves in the sun, shivering in the snow, or walking against a strong wind.

Thematic Activities

◆ Talk about the different kinds of weather that children experience throughout the year. Divide the class into groups and let each group prepare a collage of magazine pictures showing people dressed for snowy weather, rainy weather, windy weather and hot weather.

◆ Talk about the different kinds of materials that clothing is made from, such as cotton, corduroy, wool, leather, and silk. Display samples of each kind of material. Let the children feel each piece and tell whether it is heavy or light. See if they can identify the material of the clothing they are wearing.

BOOKS ARE GREAT!

CHORUS:
Books are great! Books are fun!
Books let you do what you've never done!
Books are cool! Books are in!
Books let you go where you've never been!

Read a good mystery, solve a crime!
Read about history, go back in time!
Read about outer space, land on Mars!
Read about an auto race, zoom with the cars!

CHORUS

Read about a haunted house, shake to your knees!
Read about a cat and mouse, run for the cheese!
Read about a lost dog, where can it be?
Read about a giant frog under the sea!

CHORUS

Read a very funny book, blues go away!
Read a bright, sunny book on a rainy day!
Read a goodnight book, just before bed,
Let a sleep-tight book dance in your head!

CHORUS

Suggestions for Sharing

◆ Let the children recite the chorus together, but assign individual lines for the verses. Give each child a book to hold. As each line of the poem is recited, let the children turn a page of their books, as if they were reading them.

◆ Let the children dress in costumes to represent the possible characters in their books. For example, the child reciting the line about the mysteries might dress in a detective's hat. Encourage children to perform the actions that the characters in their books might do, such as looking through a detective's magnifying glass.

Thematic Activities

◆ Take a survey to learn what kind of books the children like to read most (mysteries, adventure stories, comedies, etc.). Display the results in a bar graph or a chart. Encourage volunteers to describe favourite books they've read.

◆ Let the class visit your school library, and show them where different types of books can be located. Older children should learn how to use the card index or computer to locate books by their titles, authors, or subject matter. Let each child choose one book to read and report on later. Keep a large chart that tallies how many books the class has read throughout the year.